HEART MAKEOVER

C. LILEY MCCONNELL

Copyright © 2014 by Clem McConnell

All right reserved

This book or part thereof may not be reproduced in any form, stored in a retrieval system, or transmitted in any form by any means - electronic, mechanical, photocopy, recording, or otherwise - without prior written permission of the publisher, except as provided by the U.S. A. copyright law. An excerpt for brief quotations in critical reviews or articles is permitted.

First U.S. Printing, 2014

All Scriptures quotations are from the King James Version Bible

Library of Congress Control Number:2014950565

1. Finding Your Purpose 2. Heart Journey 3. Emotional Healing

Heart Makeover / C. Liley McConnell 1st ed.

Includes Bibliographical references

ISBN 978-0-9673490-2-2

Publishing by Healing Hearts Books. Products are available at special quantity discounts for bulk purchase. For details, write:

Healing Hearts Books at P.O. Box 97271, Raleigh, NC 27624.

healheartsbooks@aol.com

Printed by Tien Wah Press, Singapore

Cover Design by Wanda Foster

I dedicate this book to all my children at Lion of Judah and their children's children.

Isaiah 54:1 Sing, O barren, thou that didst not bear; break forth into singing, and cry aloud, thou that didst not travail with child: for more are the children of the desolate than the children of the married wife, saith the LORD.

Thank you for being an answered prayer and a manifested promise that a barren woman can have many children to love, encourage and share out of the treasure of life's goodness and God's grace. God has divinely connected our hearts to cultivate our lives with healing.

I love your laughter, creativity, and unconditional love. Thank you for allowing the Lord to unlock the songs in your heart, dance in your feet, and vision to see beyond generational, cultural, and racial limitations. You belong to Jesus and nothing is impossible with God.

Thank you for all those weekends you could have been serving yourself, but you learned the reward of serving others. You are great leaders because you are learning how to be great servants. May you walk humbly with the Lord all the days of your life and experience the great destiny He has designed for you.

You are Loved, Accepted, and Wanted....this is the L.A.W. I am so proud of you.

Love,
Ms. Liley

ACKNOWLEDGMENTS

I deeply appreciate all the time, sacrifice and support of so many who helped to make this book possible. Especially,....

To the Lord Jesus for birthing this book within my spirit to share with total transparency that you are the healer to every heart disorder. Thank you for all that you have done and are doing in me. I am grateful You would take this fragmented life and beautify it to bring You glory.

To my parents, Roy and Evelean. I honor you. Thank you for your wisdom, faith and love. You are a blessing and I appreciate you more and more each day. Thanks for your sacrifices and never giving up on me.

To Elton and Vivian, Thanks for providing beautiful accommodations over the years during the writing of this project. Your gifts were the secret places to pour out my soul, bear my heart, and bring healing.

To Mary and Clinton. Thanks for the tedious and long hours you sacrificed to edit this book. You are a blessing and I love you!

To Pastor Joy Howell. Thanks for your friendship, wisdom and leadership. Thank you for the example you are as a woman after God's heart who encourages us to pursue Him.

To all the people who have been an inspirational part of my life and become part of my heart's journey....Thank you! God meant it all for my good. May He be glorified.

CONTENTS

FOREWORD BY JOY HOWELL

REVIEWS

INTRODUCTION

1. ENTERING THE CHAMBERS......................11
2. ENTER AT YOUR OWN RISK........................17
3. WHAT'S LOVE GOT TO DO WITH IT?............23
4. BACK TO THE DRAWING BOARD..................31
5. Ssssssss...39
6. DIVINE RESTORATION..................................50
7. LIES, LIES, FATHER OF LIES..........................63
8. THE THRONE ROOM...................................73
9. DIVINE DIRECTION.....................................81

CHAMBER INVENTORY WORKSHEET

About the Author & Music

Foreword

There are people you will meet in the world who will have an impact on your life...Liley happens to be one of those people. The first time I met her she made a profound impact on me and aroused a desire in me to become her friend. I can say that I am grateful for her friendship and the privilege to work beside her in the Kingdom of God.

In her book, *Heart Makeover*, I was thrilled by the openness of Liley's heart. I was touched by the tenderness of the Father and His attention to detail in restoring each chamber of her heart. And I was provoked by the Holy Spirit to examine each area of my own heart.

This is a day where people struggle with identity and are confused with many lies that the enemy has propagated. In this book you will find honesty, truth, and power to help you begin a journey with the Lord, which will reveal truth, expose lies, release freedom, and empower you to understand your own identity in Christ.

In reading, I encourage you to take your time and enjoy; allow the Holy Spirit to walk you through the chambers of your own heart; be honest with yourself; and log your results. Allow God to set you free of the lies that have held you captive in your own heart and allow Him to define who you were created to become!

With sincere honor, respect, and love,

Joy Howell

Pastor, Church on the Rock Training Ministry

Reviews

This book is an awesome display of the Father's love and just how involved He desires to be in our lives. It will bring hope and encouragement to those who have been hurt in life and need deep inner healing.

Although the Holy Spirit deals with individuals in many ways, I do believe this could be a method that could be used by others.

I love that the book shows that God not only removes the things in our lives that are not of Him, but he replaces those things with exactly what we need. This is also a great example of how encounters with God can change us forever.

David Walston
Associate Pastor, Church on the Rock Training Ministry
Goldsboro, NC

I found this book refreshing, honest, transparent, and full of truth. I felt my own heart being cleansed as I journeyed into her encounter with the Lord. I was challenged to seek the Lord afresh and pray, "Search my heart Lord, ... There is a clarion call to get to the heart of the matter and deal with the matters of the heart.

I believe you hold in your hand a powerful tool in aiding you in your journey to establish His throne in the center of your heart, and your life as the dwelling place for His presence. What joy awaits those who answer His call!

Jonathan Chavous
Director, CORE Ministry Bible College
Church on the Rock Training Ministry
Goldsboro, NC

Introduction

Therefore judge nothing before the time, until the Lord come, who both will bring to light the hidden things of darkness, and will make manifest the counsels of the hearts: and then shall every man have praise of God. 1 **Corinthians 4:5**

I love the story of the woman at the well in John 4 as Jesus asks her to go and get her husband. Although Jesus knew her despairing state from multiple marriages, He did not condemn her with the obvious question of why did she marry five men or why was she shacking up with someone who was not her husband. Being a gentleman- He gave her the choice to reveal or hide the secret place of her heart. I believe because she answered Him with complete transparency and truth, the Lord chose to reveal Himself as the Messiah. Her encounter with Truth prepared her heart to make and exchange, expose her need for the Saviour and propel her into purpose. This was a pivotal point in her ability to go forward unburdened with the guilt and shame of her past.

As with the woman at the well, the unveiling of my divine purpose began in 2006 with a personal journey through my heart by the Holy Spirit. In the visions, the Holy Spirit displayed the heart as a home consisting of many rooms, which I will refer to as chambers. He revealed the purpose of each chamber and how its condition impacts our lives when it is in order or disorder. The most intriguing part of the journey was discovering the function of each chamber that is a foundation for the passions we pursue within His divine plan.

On this journey, the Holy Spirit exposed areas of my heart where the spiritual clutter of sin defiled God's original intent for each chamber. In Mark 7: 18-23, Jesus emphasized that it is not the things we eat with unwashed hands that defiles us, but the inward condition of the human heart. As I was studying this scripture, the Holy Spirit shared that *"within the heart of man lies all kinds of evil desires to do wrong instead of following God's righteous way. When a man follows the evil (desire) of his heart, he is moving away from the living God to a form of idolatry. Knowing your heart helps you to know God. Because when a man seeks to please Him with his heart, he is going in the right direction (away) from iniquity, shame and guilt. If the heart is void of the Word (incorruptible Truth), it is filled with flesh (corruption)."*

When we release the clutter of our heart to the Lord and repent, He does not leave us empty. He immediately makes an exchange by cleansing and restoring our soul with His goodness, grace, light and love. What a great exchange!

Like the woman at the well, an encounter with Truth began removing the barrier of sin, shame and guilt. Jesus revived hope to an outcast woman whose revealed purpose brought restoration and healing within her and overflowed into her community. I am so grateful the Holy Spirit not only revealed the inner chambers of my heart for my own healing, but with the purpose of healing others.

What the Lord has revealed in the chambers of my heart has become a framework for my life's passions, purpose, identity, and destiny's call that remains unchanged in the midst of circumstances or seasons. I confess that I am not fully walking in every aspect of the renovation and revelation. However, I acknowledge the great steps made purposefully to pursue God's heart with my heart.

I pray that as you read this book, you will pursue a personal journey to seek out your true heart's condition- not with the mind or reasoning, but with the Holy Spirit. Jesus, The Creator, has the original blueprint of your life's purpose imprinted within the chambers of your heart. Recognizing the need for an examination is the first step of the heart makeover journey.

Heart Makeover

My Will...Be Done

Jeremiah 17:9 *The heart is deceitful above all things, and desperately wicked: who can know it?*

As I sat to talk to the Lord on a warm October day in 2006, I felt a need to examine myself and I asked the Lord, "How do you feel about me?" Naturally, I wanted the Lord to lavish me with compliments about how much He loves me, how faithful and obedient I had been. I braced myself for the truth, but I was not prepared for these words... *"There is sin in your heart."*...

From that day I struggled to know what sin was lurking in my heart. I repented daily with the general plea to forgive known and unknown sin. I felt this generic line cleared the air, but a theme kept coming up when I talked to the Lord. It was a theme of *"my will"*. How could this be? I was so careful to pray about every decision and ask about details. Where was I missing it?

This sin of *"my will"* was an unanswerable question in my mind. I was sometimes overwhelmed with grief and confusion. I cried out to the Lord, but I could not comprehend what He was telling me. I felt I was doing what He told me, but all the while the echoing voice was saying *"my will"*. What is your will God? I hesitated to question Him again, but I needed clarity and confirmation.

Sunday Morning Blues

Isaiah 29:13 *Wherefore the Lord said, Forasmuch as this people draw near me with their mouth, and with their lips do honour me, but have removed their heart far from me, and their fear toward me is taught by the precept of men:*

In a dream, I saw the man sitting across the table from me saying, *"You are in danger of judgment for speaking from your mouth and not your heart."* It was a Sunday morning that I awoke to fresh numbing echo of His words in my thoughts. What was happening in my heart? I realized anyone could quote scriptures, speak Christianese and have a form of godliness. Where had my mind overruled the intentions of my heart to love the Lord? When did my heart disengage from walking with Christ by faith into mental ascension and lifeless chatter? I had to know....

It was a windy Fall day as I hurried to church. I entered the sanctuary and joined in the worship. It was one of the few times I found it hard to enter in the presence of God. I lifted my hands as if I was begging God to rescue me from this inner turmoil. I needed answers. What did the dream mean? A sweet song was played that brought tears to my face. It reminded me that Jesus left His kingdom to come die for me. A deep feeling of gratitude overwhelmed me. I cried, "Thank you Jesus for your love. Help me to love you back with my heart, not my mouth."

Today's message highlighted how God has a perfect plan to help us achieve life's goals. We can walk in His divine will and achieve the goals with His blessing; or refuse change, don't ask God, take matters in our own hands and enjoy a short lived success. God can deposit the goal, but it requires we change to walk in it. It made sense. I was convicted of my sin and was convinced more than ever that I needed to find out God's will for my life.

Today I wanted to run to the altar for prayer, but there was only an altar call for salvation. I thought I needed prayer, but the greater need was time to search my own heart before God. I didn't need someone to pray a generic blessing and send me away pacified. I walked to my car and reviewed my notes from the sermon and how I could practically apply these principles. I went through each step and begin to cry out to God. I scribbled this prayer through my tears as I sat in the parking lot sobbing.

Lord, I commit every area of my life to your plan. I erase the slate and clear the table of my plans. I ask you to come take the reigns of my life, heart, money, business, ministry and personal goals.

He Was Just Getting Started

Proverbs 4:23 *Keep thy heart with all diligence; for out of it are the issues of life.*

I was ready for change. I was tired of living a mediocre lukewarm life. God put boldness and excellence in me, yet I was far from that standard. I knew something was not right, but where was I to begin with the change. I drove home thinking of all the things I needed to finish. I wanted order and structure in every area of my life.

I begin thinking about the physical things – losing weight by exercising and changing my eating habits; cleaning the storage room, organizing my files. However, by the time I arrived home, I had cleared the slate of my agenda and plans. If I wanted to know where to start and what to do, I had to go to God. My spiritual heart problem needed attention. I could no longer remain in denial or deception.

I arrived home to have dinner with my husband and then hurried into my study room. I got on my knees and prayed for God to reveal the truth about my heart. I grabbed my note pad and for the next few hours, the Lord took me on a journey by the Spirit into my heart.

Chamber 1

Entering The Chambers

As I prayed, the Holy Spirit took me in a vision to a place inside my heart. I was amazed that my heart was built like a house. I stood inside the entrance looking down a long dimly lit hallway. I walked a few steps down the hallway to see a door on the left. I knew this was the beginning of my journey through my own heart. Although I was nervous, I trusted the Lord was guiding me through this journey. Any fear was overcome by the deeper need to know the answers that were in these chambers. I placed my hand on the door knob to enter the first chamber. I hesitated and asked God to help me with whatever was behind the door. I wanted truth no matter how bad it looked. I opened the door to the first chamber to see a naked woman dancing on a pole. It was the seductive scene one could find in any strip bar. The chamber was filled with lust.

I recalled watching a program a few months earlier based on a woman who owned a gym. I was excited to see women progress in sports since I had been involved in sports throughout my life. Before I could blink, highlights were shown of the next program with the owner in the bed with her girlfriend. I was flabbergasted! I flipped the channel quickly, but the picture was replayed over in my mind. The 3-second TV clip recalled old memories and summoned a familiar spirit that unleashed a wicked assignment of horrible dreams. I knew God had delivered me from lesbian relationships and I had no desire to return to the former lifestyle, but why was I feeling this way?

At this time, I had been happily married for four years and was faithful to my husband. However, we both bought the huge luggage of our past into the marriage. He knew before we married that I been a victim of rape, assault, and was submerged in sexual immorality. It had been five years prior to marriage that God delivered me from a nine-year cycle of bisexuality.

Through researching my genealogy, I discovered bisexuality lurking in my bloodline that could be traced to at least four generations. This tendency did not start with me but I became a victim of this "hidden" cycle of iniquity. Within days of the TV clip incident, I went to Florida on a routine business trip and reserved a room at my usual motel chain. When I arrived at the motel late that night, I noticed two adult entertainment bars directly across the street. I was too tired to find another hotel after hours of driving on the road. The temptation of lust was the strongest it had ever been since I was delivered from sexual immorality. I heard a voice say, *"No one will ever know"*. I had been traveling for many years, but this was the first time the thought of committing a sexual act outside of marriage ever crossed my mind. I knew this was a battle and I was not going to give into for any reason. Over the next few weeks, lustful thoughts came but I stayed faithful or was I?

Matthew 5:28 *But I say unto you, That whosoever looketh on a woman to lust after her hath committed adultery with her already in his heart.*

The Holy Spirit revealed years later that adultery is more than physical, but it is the exchange of His love for another. This is spiritual whoredom. He noted that the Lord has a spiritual covenant with His people and we belong to Him. This is marriage, but seeking other lovers is whoredom that leads to idolatry.

This chamber was entertaining the lustful desires and perversion of my heart from ungodly soul ties of my past. I felt sex was never the objective in most of my relationships, but the by-product of an unfulfilled life and wounded heart. I remember many times lying in bed crying because the intensity of passion brought an equal or greater depth of pain. This was years of relationships entangled with lust that grew out of compromise, and from hopeless attempts to find love and acceptance from people instead of from the Lord. Lust caused me to pervert my soul with anything I desired instead of trusting God for everything I needed with purity.

The Lord was showing me the immorality I denied with my mind because I had not physically committed the sexual act with my body, but in reality this perversion was still a resident of my heart.

It was years before I realized I needed to denounce the soul ties made with each of my lovers. The Holy Spirit allowed me to see these women still had access to my heart because of the exchange made in the spirit. They still claimed possession, control, and influence to enter back in my life disguising their stronghold as friendship. Now I fully understood how the small foxes spoil the vine.

As I looked in the room, I did the only thing I knew that could help me. I repented and cried out to the Lord.

Lord, I confess the lust in my heart. I ask you to forgive me. Create in me a clean heart and renew a right spirit within me. Cleanse me with Your blood. I will not walk in the flesh, but be led by Your Spirit. Spirit of lust, I give you no place in my heart. I denounce you in Jesus' Name.

It was over. I don't remember walking out of the room or closing the door, but now I was standing in the hallway. I noticed directly across the hall from the first chamber was another door on my right side. It was time to open the door and enter another chamber of my heart.

Heart Makeover

Chamber 2

Enter At Your Own Risk

I was ready to see what could possibly be next. I poised myself, put my hand on the doorknob, opened the door and peeked in the door. The noise coming out of this room sounded too familiar. I could hear my husband and I quarreling. I don't know what we were fighting about, but it was obvious this room was full of strife.

Harold, an Irish and Native American Indian, and I, an African American, had been married almost four years. I was 39 years old when I married for the first time and my husband was thirteen years older. This was his second marriage after 20 years of being divorced. He was a great provider and loved Jesus. We would spend time reading The Bible and worshiping in the house together. However, the difference in our age and culture caused some issues of insecurity and control throughout our marriage.

I also entered this union with my own set of issues, to include my sense of rejection and abandonment. This caused me not to trust anyone nor feel accepted. It did not help that my husband and I both suffered from deep rooted bitterness. We both were set in our ways, but we knew God had ordained our marriage. It was the becoming "one flesh" thing that was challenging. Some days we had very loud discussions that the neighbors could hear.

I can honestly say I loved my husband, but I had a problem with my temper since I was very young. Although I have stopped fighting with my fist, I was still pretty effective with my words. I would get angry and lash out. It didn't help that we were both stubborn. I was raised to be an independent do-it-yourself woman. I wasn't sure how far this submission thing had to go. In my efforts to submit, I held inside all the things that bothered me and let them build up. This was unhealthy and unwise. Eventually, the days would come when I could hold in no more. I would release a barrage of words in an effort to defend myself against every accusation and criticism.

The first two years of this union, I prayed for God to deliver me from the anger. One day the Lord spoke to me about my anger issue. He explained that the anger was only a symptom of a deeper rooted problem of unforgiveness and bitterness. The unforgiveness creates a bond of control and fear with the offending person. As of result, I became like the person with whom I was offended. Instead of faith to trust in God, faith is used to focus on the offense, which strengthens bitter roots in the heart. I spent many years praying for God to take away my anger, not realizing it was only a leaf on the tree of a deeper rooted issue.

This room was displaying the strife I was entertaining in my heart.

God was not pleased. I stood with my eyes cast down. The sounds were easy to recognize because they echoed sounds I had sometimes heard in my childhood. They were hostile, mean, and cutting words. The cycle was being replayed. I had been an "emotional mute" since my early childhood. This is a term I created to describe my inability to communicate my feelings in a manner that could be expressed, understood, and valued as true. Somehow, I came to the conclusion that the only acceptable way to express my pain was in the extreme emotions of silence, tears, or anger. Just because I had obtained a higher tolerance level to not quarrel now that I was a married adult, did not mean I was living with peace in my heart. The absence of violence is not the measure of peace. The Lord was showing me the sin I continued to carry in my heart.

Proverbs 17:1 *Better is a dry morsel, and quietness therewith, than an house full of sacrifices with strife.*

The answer to uproot strife, anger, and unforgiveness is to pull down the thoughts of offense before they stir emotions in my heart. I had to confess my sin and forgive my enemy through prayer. As I looked in the room, I repented and cried out to the Lord in a prayer that went something like this.

Lord, I confess the strife in my heart. I ask you to forgive me. Create in me a clean heart and renew a right spirit within me. Cleanse me with Your blood. The fruit of Your Spirit is love, peace and joy. Spirit of strife, anger, bitterness, I give you no place in my heart. I evict you in Jesus' Name. Lord, I ask You to cleanse me of all unrighteousness Prince of Peace, come in this chamber of my heart and abide in me.

It was over. With each room, I felt a weight off my soul. I felt ready to move to the next room.

Chamber 3

What's Love Got To Do With It?

I was encouraged by the process and feeling the change from evicting some unwelcome guests. The momentum of repentance and change was far more desirable than holding back for fear of truth. Before I opened the door, I heard the Holy Spirit say, *"There are four more doors"*.
I drew the chambers on my yellow notepaper and labeled the two chambers I had already entered. There were a total of seven chambers. In scripture, the number seven represents perfection and completeness. This is an awesome picture to signify the perfect wholeness of a heart designed by God.

I reflected on how I had helped someone clean a two story house. We had been working for almost two hours. I thought we were done until another door was opened that led to the kids' playroom. I refocused my mind and sighed as I continued to clean another hour. This is how I felt about the heart chambers. I knew this was going to be a long process. I was nowhere near the end.

It was easy to open the door to the third chamber. I did not understand what I was seeing, but it made me sad. I could see a woman hanging from the ceiling. She had a rope tied around her neck. The best I

Heart Makeover

could tell, she was dead. Before I could ask, I heard the Holy Spirit say, *"self-hatred, suicide."* I wanted to weep, but there was no time. I had to search the mental files to find out what opened the door to this murderous spirit.

According to Wikipedia, self-hatred (also called self-loathing) refers to an extreme dislike or hatred of oneself, or being angry at or even prejudiced against oneself. Self-hatred and shame are important factors in many mental disorders, especially disorders that involve a perceived defect of oneself. Self-hatred is also a symptom of many personality disorders, including borderline personality disorder and depression. The Oxford English Dictionary defines suicide as the action of killing oneself intentionally. This includes a course of action that is disastrously damaging to oneself or one's own interests.

I will make this clear-I do not believe in suicide, but I entertained the idea as a way of escape from hopelessness and immense pain. It is never the answer to any situation, but in my depressed state of mind my heart was open to its beckoning calls. I believe part of this story for this chamber started when I was in my early twenties. This was the first time suicidal thoughts seriously came to my mind. I had been saved since I was 14 years old, but had my first encounter with the Holy Spirit when I was about 18 years old. This is when I had such zeal to seek the Lord in a deeper place through a personal relationship and not based on external family pressures. I was on fire for God and had begun living for Him.

out of the bed and ran out of the balcony door. As I looked for a place to jump to safety, my attacker pulled me away from the railing and flung my body against the cement wall. He placed the gun to my head to invoke fear so I would bow to his will as he tried to pull me in the bedroom. My mind raced back to the previous rape only four years ago. I did not think about dying or being shot, but only avoiding the pain of being raped. I resisted his force as I called out to the darkness of night, "Fire!" hoping someone would come to my rescue. There we were in what felt like an eternity on the balcony with our wills gridlocked in idleness. Why? That is all I wanted to know. Why? Somewhere in the lifeless chatter, his gesture gave him away and I discovered it was my neighbor. I called his name and he fled leaving me to sink beneath the sea of his cruelty on the balcony.

The ordeal ended as a farmer came to my rescue and called the police. There was no suppressing the pain or hiding the evidence this time. I had to file a police report and testify in trial against my attacker. During the court proceedings I found out that my attacker had invited two of his friends to join him that night to gang rape me, but they declined the invitation. The Lord was still watching over me and protecting me in the midst of this foiled rape attempt. I thank God in realizing the attack could have been worse if his friends would have joined him and maybe they would have succeeded. Even in my backslidden state, God had protected me. However, this trauma brought me to my knees in utter despair. My wall of distrust grew taller and prevented anyone from helping me. I believed the lie that sex was all I was good for, and I had to stop this cycle of pain. I bought a 9mm gun, loaded it, and slept with it in my arms for many weeks after the incident. I did not leave my room. By the grace of God, my girlfriend would take off from work, sit beside my bed and read The Bible to me. I remember hearing her read the Psalms from the Word of God becoming the source of life that gave me the strength to live.

I finally gained the strength to leave my room. I then faced the next enemy of my soul. I know what happened to me was not my fault, but through the eyes of the police, my employer, and my co-workers, I was to blame. The police reported that the man was my boyfriend and my employer noted that what I was wearing seduced him, despite the fact that I was in bed sleep.

Although God gave me strength to get through the slander, accusations, and criticism, it did not change how I felt about myself. I reached out to someone I loved dearly for comfort, but their advice was that I should, "get over it", echoed long and hard through my soul. I pressed my pain deep down inside and tried to forget the night I embraced death on the balcony.

Although it had taken years to forgive the man who violated and perhaps intended to kill me, I had not forgiven myself. There would be intermittent seasons of suicidal ideation and attempts. I do not believe that these series of traumas caused self-hatred, but became the fertile ground for the seed to grow. I must clarify that I do not believe in suicide. I do not believe it is God's will for us to self-murder. However, because of the prevailing self-hatred in my heart from unresolved traumas, this led to a depressed state of mind that opened the door to suicide's invitation to end it all. I can recall two other situations where I would have taken my life if it were not for divine intervention.

I stood in the door of the third room of my heart chamber revisiting my memories, which were clouded with years of pain and sorrow. I did not know suicide and self-hatred still lingered in my heart waiting for another deadly blow of emotional turmoil to destroy my life. I held my head up with sadness in my eyes; I repented and cried out to the Lord.

Lord, I confess the spirit of suicide and self-hatred in my heart. I ask you to forgive me. You formed me in my mother's womb and know my inner most thoughts. I am fearfully and wonderfully made. I declare I shall not die, but live and declare the works of the Lord. You came that I might have life more abundantly.

Create in me a clean heart and renew a right spirit within me. Cleanse me with Your blood. Spirit of suicide and self-hatred, you have no place in my heart. I evict you in Jesus' Name. I ask You to cleanse me of all unrighteousness. Prince of Peace, come in this chamber of my heart and abide in me. I submit to Your will.

Chamber 4

Back to the Drawing Board

It was time to enter the next chamber. I quickly opened the door to see a young woman sitting in a room with the window open. As she faced the window, there was a drawing easel in front of her. She was drawing on large flip chart paper. I could not see what she was drawing but her face showed her displeasure. I began to analyze what this room could represent. Then it came clearer as I spoke, *"She was drawing…drawing…drawing for attention."* Her face displayed her disappointment and frustration that no one noticed her work.

I searched my thoughts to see where I felt like the center of attention. I thought I was used to attention, but maybe I wasn't. I was the middle child in a middle-class family. I noticed that the first born was loved and cherished. My parents proudly displayed several of my older sister's pictures in the family photo albums. However, there were no baby pictures of me adorning the hallowed pages of our family photos albums. It was like I was born and forgotten. Although my parents deny it, my 5 year old mind concluded that I was adopted. In the earliest photo I remember, I was about 3 years old.

Then my youngest sibling was born. He was the last child and the long awaited first boy. I remember my sister and I listening on the phone as someone announced his birth. There was such excitement in the house about my baby brother and we loved him. God in His infinite wisdom blessed me with a brother born on my birthday exactly six years apart. I could no longer be forgotten. There was a reason to celebrate my birthday because it was shared with my only brother.

After years of healing in my adulthood, I have tried ways to put the pieces together that surrounded my birth. I was told that in the 1960s, pregnant women did not attend school because it was not socially accepted, whether you were married or not. Because of this written code of conduct, my mother had to drop out of college when she became pregnant with me. I learned that while I was in the womb, there was an altercation between my parents that deeply wounded my mother. I was told that from the time of my birth, I cried almost continuously as an infant. I must have felt I was an unwanted reminder of her pain. It seemed my birth was preceded by a series of great disappointments that caused my mother great emotional turmoil.

I know my mother loved me, but she also made great strides to criticize, belittle, accuse, and provoke me to anger. I knew at an early age that I did not want children because I felt that I was a mistake. I viewed children as a burden because I felt like a burden. I am sad to say that before I was saved, I felt I would have aborted my child if I were ever pregnant. This was due to my twisted perception based on my own experience. I thank God that He never allowed me to have children that I may have killed in my selfish pain. I no longer hold any unforgiveness toward my mother. I realized she was hurting, and we can only share with others what is in our heart.

My mother and I were not close during my early years and my father was gone frequently with his job. My mother nurtured my siblings and they were very close, but I felt emotionally abandoned and became physically isolated. When I was in my forties, I found my only baby picture in a photo album. It was so mangled that I could not remove it from the photo album without tearing it. It looked like it had been balled up and then flattened out to be displayed with shame. This only affirmed the deep seed of rejection embedded in my soul.

In 2004, the Lord showed me a vision of when I was an infant lying in the crib crying. He allowed me to see my mother standing in the doorway staring at me. She had a look of disgust and resentment on her face. Though I cried for her to come, she would not enter the room. In the vision, I turned to the wall and continued to cry for attention. Suddenly, I saw the Lord Jesus was standing over my crib. He smiled at me letting me know He heard my cry and He came to comfort my lonely soul. Without knowing this in my conscious mind, I recognized that throughout my life I would lie in bed, turn to the wall and just cry…waiting for someone to love me…waiting for attention.

Maybe I was begging for attention by overachieving in everything I did. I had to prove I was just as, "loved and wanted" as my siblings.

Heart Makeover

My mother told me when I was very young that, *"you'll never make it."* In my mind, I had to prove through performance that I was worthy of my parent's acceptance. It made me over-compensate for the lack of attention because of my father's distractions with work and my mother's wounding words. I learned to remain isolated and accept this as my badge of courage to avoid rejection and disapproval. I would drift away in the world of my imagination. This was good for my creativity, but crippling to deal with reality.

After I graduated from college, I immediately went into the military and was assigned overseas. It had become so unbearable at home that I had to check into a hotel to avoid the scathing verbal attacks and blame as a scapegoat when my brother broke a bone in his arm playing football. I wanted to get as far away from my mother and my past as I could. The Lord shared with me years later that He opened the door for me to enter the military as a way of escape from the emotional abuse I had endured for years. Although I may never fully understand why I became the recipient of my mother's pain, I have no resentment against her. I love my mother and pray the Lord will heal her in those broken places of her life.

However, on the flip side, I performed to prove I was worth loving. I was performing for my father's acceptance. I deeply love my father and always wanted to measure up to his high standards – which I believed I never could achieve. I perceived my father's motives for me to perform were to see me do well and be successful. He has always placed a high regard on excellence in everything and to strive for perfection. However, the downfall of trying to be a perfectionist is being overcritical of myself and others, instead of celebrating their success with acceptance.

<u>I am blessed to have both of my parents healthy and living over 70 years of age. I am grateful for all their sacrifices and love. I honor them for never leaving me through all those tough times. What I am sharing is not to dishonor them, but to relate why there was a drawing for attention.</u>

In my adulthood, the Holy Spirit took me to a time when I was about 7 years old sitting on the ground behind a bush in the front yard. I remember this day that I felt so alone and was questioning my identity. In the vision, Jesus came and sat beside me. I told Him…*"Lord, I feel so alone. They didn't want me. They wanted a boy."* I felt this messed with my identity. I didn't know who I was and who I had become was not good enough.

Jesus responded to my pain. I heard Him say *"I was there. I was with you all the time… protecting you…loving you. I was there. I know who you are. You are My daughter. That is all you need to know. I will never leave nor forsake you. I have never. When you don't know who you are, you are easily taken in by others. Pain- I did not give that to you. It is a lie of the enemy. You are wanted."* I tell the Lord that it still feels true that although my mother didn't abort me, she didn't want me.

Heart Makeover

In the vision, I saw Jesus kneel in front of the seven year old child and say *"Look at Me."* I held my head down and responded *"I can't Lord, I am so ashamed."* Slowly I raised my head to look in His eyes and see radiant light. He said, *"There is nothing but love and acceptance from the Father. I have been here all the time. I accept you. I love you."* The lie surfaced to remind me of the betrayal I experienced from those I trusted. I heard a voice say, *"You must fend for yourself"* and *"No one will take care of you but you."* I looked at Jesus and asked Him was that true. Jesus said to me, *"It is not true. I have always been there.... count the ways."*

Many foiled accidents and incidents that happened throughout my life flashed through my mind. He reminded me He was on the balcony and at the door. This was the balcony of the attempted rape and assault with a gun discussed in the previous chapter. He was at the door of the house to prevent the other two men from joining him and at the bedroom door to prevent my attacker from pulling me inside.

I still had questions about my identity and I asked Jesus why I went through a nine year cycle of bisexuality. I heard Jesus say, *"It was not about being gay (lesbian). It was about being accepted....your identity."* I wept because through all of the relationships I was seeking something I did not find in men or women, black or white, rich or poor. They could never give me the truth of my own identity and fill the need for acceptance.

I saw in this chamber a woman who had not dealt with the wounds of her own rejection, condemnation and inferiority. There was no joy in the face of this woman drawing. What joy could come from being self-absorbed or self-centered? This attention she longed to have still left her empty. Now it was time to refocus. I repented prayerfully to the Lord.

Lord, I repent of drawing attention and seeking vainglory in my heart. Forgive me for wanting the applause of men to mask the fear of rejection. I ask you to forgive me for pride and self-centeredness. You resist the proud, but lift humble. Forgive me for determining my value based on the approval or attention of man. Forgive me for not being content having Your attention, Your favor, and Your presence. I repent Father for drawing attention to myself instead of You. You be lifted up in my life that through me, many are drawn to You.

Create in me a clean heart and renew a right spirit within me. Cleanse me with Your blood. Spirit of pride, self-centeredness that draws attention, you have no place in my heart. I evict you in Jesus' Name. The blood of Jesus flows in my heart. I ask you to cleanse me of all unrighteousness. I humble myself to You King of Glory. Come in this chamber of my heart.

I turned away from the woman to walk out the door. Before I could take a step the occupant of the next chamber stood in the doorway.

Heart Makeover

Chamber 5 Ssssssss…..

2 Corinthians 11:3 But I fear, lest by any means, as the serpent beguiled Eve through his subtlety, so your minds should be corrupted from the simplicity that is in Christ.

There was no time to approach the door of Chamber 5. The sound of my footsteps or the power of the prayer summoned an aggressive unexpected intruder. This was not the moment to be fearful. I gazed up at a large cobra-like snake. Its' head was as wide as the door and its body stretched outside the door of Chamber 5. I begin speaking the Word of God. *"You vile serpent, you have no place or power in my heart."* I started walking toward the snake. Every time I took a step, it withdrew to the 5th chamber. When we were both inside the room, the snake coiled it body tightly to fit. I stood face to face with the enemy of my heart and soul.

James 3:6 And the tongue is a fire, a world of iniquity: so is the tongue among our members, that it defileth the whole body, and setteth on fire the course of nature; and it is set on fire of hell. (KJV)

An attribute of a snake is that it has poison in its mouth (fangs). It is the tongue the book of James tells the believer to take great strides to tame. I realize I was being shown that when I have failed to tame my tongue, I have injured others and defiled the <u>whole</u> body. This goes beyond my physical body with sickness and my soul with emotional anguish, but it carries over to the spiritual body, the church.

As proven in the previous chambers, it was through the Word of God that this serpent could be tamed. I had seen enough at this point to know every spirit exposed had to leave in Jesus' Name. I only had two more rooms to enter and I was not turning back now. I began praying:

Jesus I repent of this hateful, mean spirit in my heart. You are the God of love, let Your love overtake every spirit of enmity. You gave Your love to me while I was yet a sinner. God I give my love to You. I will honor You by loving You with my heart, mind, soul and strength. Please forgive me Jesus. I repent for hurting You and others with hateful words and actions. Forgive me for my sin, transgression, and iniquity.

Create in me a clean heart and renew a right spirit within me. Cleanse me with Your blood of this spirit of control, manipulation, witchcraft, meanness, wickedness, and hatred. I repent for ten generations in my father's and mother's bloodline. This spirit will not curse our family any longer. We will walk in the blessing of God. Serpent, you have no place in my heart. Jesus, let the light of Your love and Your pure blood flow in my heart. I ask You to cleanse me of all unrighteousness. Come in this chamber of my heart.

Suddenly the snake was gone. The chamber was filled with light. The chamber now had a white bathtub in the middle of the room with a brush. I looked inside to see the clear water. I love to take baths and fill them with sweet fragrances. I had not done this in a long time. John 15:3 says, *"Now ye are clean through the word which I have spoken unto you."* We are forgiven through Christ's blood but we are washed through His Word. Just as there is a need for daily bathing, so it is necessary to bathe in the Word of God. The Holy Spirit not only reveals our sin, but guides us to repent daily for impurities in heart. The tongue once yielded to sin that brought the curse of death, now becomes an instrument of life and peace. The bath represents a place of cleansing, purification and washing, nakedness and healing. I felt the Lord was telling me this part of my heart was a safe place again. I could trust Him. Where the serpent had resided and distorted purpose, the Lord had restored this chamber to its original design.

Hebrews 10:22 *says, "Let us draw near with a true heart in full assurance of faith, having our hearts sprinkled from an evil conscience, and our bodies washed with pure water.*

The Lord provided the place and provision for removing the filth of an "evil conscience" polluted by sin and burdened with guilt. Notice the invitation to draw near is <u>after</u> our hearts are sprinkled and bodies are washed. We then have a quiet confidence that now allows our heart to be led by the Spirit.
.
The writer of Psalms 15:1-3 presents the question, *LORD, who shall abide in your tabernacle? who shall dwell in your holy hill? He that*

walketh uprightly, and worketh righteousness, and <u>speaks the truth</u> in his heart. He that backbiteth not with his tongue, nor does evil to his neighbor, nor taketh up a reproach against his neighbor.

The journey in this chamber continued as the focus changed to another part of the room where I was getting a full body massage. The room was filled with the fragrance of body oils.

The Old Testament provides several examples where water and oil were used. The first is in preparation for marriage.

Esther 2:12 *Now when every maid's turn was come to go in to king Ahasuerus, after that she had been twelve months, according to the manner of the women, (for so were the days of their purifications accomplished, to wit, six months with oil of myrrh, and six months with sweet odours, and with other things for the purifying of the women;)*

I was getting closer to Chamber Seven, where I knew the King would reside. All of this was preparation to enter His presence. The oils were applied after the bathing to make the skin soft and smooth. The Bible frequently uses oil and water to symbolize the Holy Spirit. And so it is with the Holy Spirit who abides within us to keep our hearts pliable and receptive to the Lord. This represents the outward cleansing and inward purity of the bride prepared for Christ.

This chamber's purpose was to focus on taking care of my whole being- body, soul and spirit. This was now the Health & Body room. Jesus performed an instant remodeling. I stood in awe. This had not happened in the other chambers or had it?

Heart Makeover

Divine Restoration

***Psalms 73:26** My flesh and my heart faileth: but God is the strength of my heart, and my portion for ever.*

I had to return to the other chambers to see how they were changed when I repented. I wanted to see what they were before they were defiled with sin and filled with darkness. I only had two more chambers to encounter on my journey, but they would have to wait for now. I began to identify each restored room by its purpose. I called Chamber 5 the Health & Body Chamber because it focused on my body as the temple of The Holy Spirit. It was my responsibility to exercise, maintain proper rest, grooming, and eating habits.

In one of the houses I lived, there was a deep, long tub that I could stretch out my long legs and enjoy relaxing under the skylight overhead. I would sit for hours and sometimes fall asleep in the soothing waters. This was my escape from the long week of physical activity. This was part of who I was and I was excited that the Lord gave me a large bathtub in my heart. The message of this room is to take care of His temple and lavishly care for it in preparation to enter the presence of The King.

I was overjoyed with excitement over the changes I observed in this chamber. I had to reenter the other rooms in reverse order to see the Lord's divine makeover.

Heart Makeover

Chamber 4 Restored

Galatians 5:13 *For, brethren, ye have been called unto liberty; only use not liberty for an occasion to the flesh, but by love serves one another.*

I walked back into the fourth chamber, where the woman had been drawing for attention. I could see the light shining through the window. I quietly watched as she was now caring for a person lying in a bed. I perceived the person lying down was sick and helpless. This woman was so attentive and gentle with the sick person. She was no longer seeking to draw attention to herself. She became a servant to the weak and needy. The self-seeking woman transformed into a selfless servant. This chamber was now the Servant-Giving Chamber.

In 2006, the Lord instructed me to return to school to get a Bachelors degree in Social Work. This was to prepare me for my next assignment because He was sending me to work with children and families. I was doing some community work with the homeless, incarcerated, and poor, but my previous degrees were business related. In obedience to His guidance, I applied to the designated university and was accepted in the social work program. By the grace and favor of God, I was accepted in the scholars program, awarded a scholarship and graduated with honors.

Heart Makeover

After graduation, I volunteered on staff at a Christian Equine program. I gained valuable experience working with families. I used my new found social work skills to interview and pray with parents, schedule riding sessions, and maintain the administrative areas for the organization. This was also a time of great healing from my own grief. (I will explain this later.) The Lord used this opportunity to prepare me for the mission field in which I would serve.

I am blessed to now work directly with families in my community where I have an opportunity to express my faith in Jesus. Although there are challenging days, I enjoy the opportunity to serve families and protect children. I have never viewed being a social worker as a job, but an ordained calling and passion from the Lord. He provides grace and compassion to encourage families in what appears to be hopeless and difficult situations. Through my own healing process, grace enables me to give attention to what matters to God –bringing hope and healing to restore families to wholeness.

The Lord led me to start working weekly with children in areas of the inner city. The program focuses on using performing arts and a biblical foundation to help children heal from trauma in high risk environments. The Lord has been faithful to give favor with the community, provision for the ministry, and growth in the number of children impacted.

Out of my own emotional experiences, the Lord is allowing me to encourage these children with the great love and acceptance Jesus has for them. In their healing process, the children are learning the joy of worship and giving to others. I share with them how my life was emotionally crippled through selfishness, but how being a radical giver brings great joy and blessings. I am blessed to have the opportunity to experience the joy of teaching children in a capacity I have never imagined-as a spiritual mother.

God has a great sense of humor in allowing me at 48 years old to have children. I confess I am not the perfect mother, but even with my flaws, my children trust and love me. They know that I love them and would lay my life down for them. They are gifts from God and a manifested promise He gave me years ago that has come to pass.

***Isaiah 54:1** Sing, O barren, thou that didst not bear; break forth into singing, and cry aloud, thou that didst not travail with child: for more are the children of the desolate than the children of the married wife, saith the LORD.*

***Isaiah 54:2** Enlarge the place of thy tent, and let them stretch forth the curtains of thine habitations: spare not, lengthen thy cords, and strengthen thy stakes;*

Chamber 3 Restored

Psalms 32:11 *Be glad in the LORD, and rejoice, ye righteous: and shout for joy, all ye that are upright in heart.*

I peeped in the door to see the chamber full of light. I saw a woman who looked like me sitting in a chair and writing. The writer looked up and waved her right hand. The expression on her face was of total joy. She loved what she was doing. She was writing books. I heard a noise in the corner of the room. There was a small television on but there was no picture displaying on the fuzzy screen. I concluded that there was no cable or satellite service. The message was clear that the writing could not be distracted with television. I stepped back to leave and the writer looked up again, smiled and waved excitedly…goodbye.

The suicidal and self-hatred chamber was now the Writing Chamber. My restored sense of purpose gave me a joy for life where death dwelled to destroy me. I was created to be a writer. Many had prophesied that I would write several books. Now the Lord was showing me Himself. He had put an entire chamber in my heart to write books. Of all the rooms so far, I felt the most joy in this chamber. In 2007, the Lord allowed me the honor to write, illustrate and publish my first children's book, <u>I Speak to Myself: Encouraging Words for Children</u>. In 2010, the Lord blessed me with a second book called <u>Raindrops of Mercy: Comforting Words for Children.</u>

Although this book started the day of the visions in 2006, it has taken years of removing layers of hurt and receiving healing to share from a place of gratitude and not bitterness. When the Lord told me after the vision that this would be a book, He shared that it would bring healing to me and others.

With each review, addition and change to the book, the Lord continually poured out His grace and healing to restore the broken places. I feel no shame in bearing the darkness of my heart because Jesus did not end my story that way. John 3:17 says *For God sent not his Son into the world to condemned the world; but that the world through him might be saved.* Jesus revealed His glorious plan and purpose that He ordained in each chamber of my heart before I was conceived.

I pray He will lead you in that place of healing and restoration as you continue this journey with me.

Chamber 2 Restored

Ephesians 5:21 *Submitting yourselves one to another in the fear of God.*

22 Wives, submit yourselves unto your own husbands, as unto the Lord.

28 So ought men to love their wives as their own bodies. He that loveth his wife loveth himself.

29 For no man ever yet hated his own flesh; but nourisheth and cherisheth it, even as the Lord the church:

33 Nevertheless let every one of you in particular so love his wife even as himself; and the wife see that she reverence her husband.

I was more excited with each divine restoration. Anticipating the revelation of the next change, I hurried to the second chamber. I saw a woman sitting in the corner sipping a cup of tea. The cup was beautifully designed with a pink flower and a gold rim. Wow! A Soothing Tea Room. Oh, how I love hot tea! It is like hot soup to my soul. I can sip, sit, and relax, as I reflect on life or enjoy time with Jesus.

This woman stood up and moved to the center of the room where my husband stood. He took her in his arms, extended their right hand to the side and they began to waltz around the room. They were enjoying each other's company. They were no longer in strife. They were romantic...

Ooh! Standing there watching with delight, I looked at the floor and saw a small snake coming to attack them. Not again! I begin speaking The Word. *"Satan, you are under my feet. You will not bring anymore strife between us. You are not welcome. Be Gone!"* Then I took my foot and crushed his head and yelled for someone to come remove him. *"Come take this out"*. I felt like angels were attending us as someone removed the dead carcass.

After this vision, I became a more attentive wife. My husband and I would play worship music and dance around the house praising the Lord. We had wonderful times together, but even in the tough times I remembered God's desire revealed in the chamber. I reached a point where I was just tired of the strife. I told Harold I would never argue with him again. The Lord taught me how to fight the spirit of strife through prayer and speaking The Word. This revelation knowledge can save you millions in counseling because it works!

I can give several examples of how the Lord honored my prayers when I honored Him in those challenging situations. I saw immediate results I came to a place where I chose to stay in peace because I was willing to submit every situation to the Lord. If I was wrong, I was able to go to my husband and ask for forgiveness and if he was wrong, the Lord had him come to me and ask for forgiveness. I learned how to let The Holy Spirit be The Referee of Peace. This removed the burden of taking on false responsibility for things out of my control. Amen!

My husband began to suffer from high blood pressure in 2008. He had been in and out of the hospital for about five months that year. Although I tried to help him, I watched him deteriorate as his heart grew weaker. He was dying and he knew it, but I did not see it coming. I watched my husband change as he stopped going to church regularly when he previously would arrive an hour before Sunday school. He was unable to work for weeks at a time and had become despondent. I was still attending college and would come home to be greeted by angry words. I still do not understand everything my husband was going through emotionally, but I had come to a place where his hurtful words and accusations did not work their intent.

I remember his last verbal attack reached so far back into my past and so deep into my soul that I physically bowed over on the floor on my knees with pain. I remember sleeping on the couch that night as I cried out to the Lord to please search my heart if I had done anything to harm my husband. I slept in great peace. It was two days before my husband asked me to forgive him. His request was with such sincerity and humility, I know it was only the grace of God that we reconciled and enjoyed the remaining week together in peace.

The next Saturday morning, he rolled over in bed to caress my left cheek with his large warm hand. He sat up on the bed and coughed up blood. As I drove him to the emergency room, my husband turned to me and said four times, "I'm going". These were the last words he spoke. He collapsed in the car less than a quarter of a mile from the emergency room. After he was admitted to the hospital, I was informed his brain had been without oxygen for a significant amount of time and he may not recover. I called his family out of state to be by his side. Within a week, he died of congestive heart failure and a lack of oxygen to his brain. My husband went to be with Jesus in April 2009 at 58 years old.

We had a wonderful memorial service and I was able to celebrate his life. He loved the Lord and that could not be denied. I am so grateful the Lord allowed us that time to get things right before he died. I will always love him. Rest in peace my husband…no more strife. Thank you for helping me to learn how to trust and enjoy greater intimacy in worship to heal emotional wounds.

In remembrance of this restored chamber of my heart of how the Lord meant it be between us, I painted the dining room pink and converted it to the Soothing Tea room where I felt complete peace.

I eventually moved from the house to be closer to school and to facilitate my own healing. It took me over a year to grieve and begin to release the pain of losing my husband. There was a lot of his belonging

Heart Makeover

to sort through. I had a lot of questions and I got a lot of answers to questions that I never knew to ask. In the end, I realize that the Lord gave me a wonderfully imperfect man who loved God and loved the wonderfully imperfect me. I appreciate the time that we spent together and I honor him as a man of faith. Thank you! It was time to move to the next room to review the last redesign.

Chamber 1 Restored

***1John 1:7** But if we walk in the light, as he is in the light, we have fellowship one with another, and the blood of Jesus Christ his Son cleanseth us from all sin.*

Remember the naked woman dancing on the pole. She was gone. The room was full of bright light. A fully clothed woman in a white dress stood in the empty room looking out of the window. I moved closer to the window to see what was capturing her attention. There was such contentment on her face. I looked out the window and saw a large light bulb. No…not a large light bulb like for a room lamp. I mean a light bulb the size of an oversized light pole. This bulb was about 20 – 25 feet tall. What did this represent?

***Genesis 1:3-4** And God said, Let there be light: and there was light. And God saw the light, that it was good: and God divided the light from the darkness.*

In Genesis God reveals light to earth that is void, chaotic, and dark before He filled the earth with life. God gave order to that which was in disorder. The first chamber of my heart is symbolically the foundation of the heart.

Just as 1 John 1 says,

5. This then is the message which we have heard of him, and declare unto you, that God is light, and in him is no darkness at all. 6. If we say that we have fellowship with him, and walk in darkness, we lie, and do not the truth: 7. But if we walk in the light, as he is in the light, we have fellowship one with another, and the blood of Jesus Christ his Son cleanses us from all sin.

As I have been allowed to revisit the chambers on my journey, the common denominator is the presence of light. However, the light did not appear until I confessed my sins and repented. It was not just entering the room, knowing what was in the room or agreeing with what I saw in the room – I had to confess my sin. It was plain and clear in my heart. There was no room for distractions or misinterpretations. I did not want the darkness, but in and of myself- nothing would have changed apart from Jesus revealed light.

9. If we confess our sins, he is faithful and just to forgive us our sins, and to cleanse us from all unrighteousness.

It is interesting that lust would pervert the pure love of God. Everything in the heart must first start with love. The purpose of the light is to shine the love of Jesus-the way, the truth, the life- in my heart. The light shows those in darkness that Christ brings freedom.

As I reflect on my younger life, the sad commentary is 80% of my close relationships were formed through sexual contact. The mark of lust is that it takes without regard for others and is predatory in nature. This spirit of lust had so marred my life through ungodly, unnatural, and other predatory experiences that violated me to resonate deep in the core of what was my innocence. Each attack, rape, assault, and perversion came out of a spirit of lust.

With the absence of godly love, we compromise the desire to love with the facade of lust. I am sad when I see so many beautiful young girls give their virginity away to be accepted, loved, or as a means of survival. They are swept up in the tide of compromise with the culture and worldliness. They have unnatural affections and lustful pleasures that dim the light of their soul and take away their sexual purity and innocence.

As I was finishing this book, I had to attend training on Child Sexual Abuse. After three days of training, I noticed I became very irritated and angry. I began to pray about this stirring in my emotions from watching videos of victims and offenders sharing their stories of sexual abuse. The training surfaced the original wound. I remembered the person who took my virginity. I remember how he made me feel stupid for not knowing what was going on and dumb for never giving me the chance to say no. I wept again with shame over my innocence being taken.

The Lord revealed how He protected me from worse harm and asked me to forgive the person who took my virginity. After 40 years, I never realized I had not forgiven him. I wept incredibly with sorrow for my innocence. I thought about how different my life may have been if this wicked seed would have never been planted in my soul. The Lord showed me this person's own brokenness and pain. So I wept for both of us, forgave them, and released the pain.

2 Corinthians 4:6 *For God, who commanded the light to shine out of darkness, hath shined in our hearts, to give the light of the knowledge of the glory of God in the face of Jesus Christ.*

Now this chamber had been restored. The fresh sense of purpose and identity permeated through my entire being. I stood there with the woman enjoying the Light, but the cleansing process was not over. It was time to get back to work in the last two chambers.

Heart Makeover

Chamber 6

Lies, Lies, Father of Lies

1John 1:8 If we say that we have no sin, we deceive ourselves, and the truth is not in us.

I walked from Chamber One to the end of the hall. I observed Chamber Six was the last chamber on the right side of the hallway. What areas of sin could remain? I felt such peace and cleanliness already established in my heart. The changes were tangible and evident. I was ready to take my heart back from the enemy and give it back to God. I opened the door and gasped. It was a six-foot tall lizard. It was standing upright. This lizard had birthed many babies. The room was filled with baby lizards climbing on the walls. This was not good. I knew a lizard symbolizes a "long tale". It was a chamber where the spirit of lying was not only living, but breeding.

Psalms 101:7 *He that worketh deceit shall not dwell within my house: he that telleth lies shall not tarry in my sight.*

There was not a lot to figure out what was going on in this chamber. I never set out to distort or hold back truth. This may have been done not to hurt someone's feelings, to make the story more sensational or to protect my pride. No matter the motive, the outcome was still sin and my heart was infested with this habit of living a lie. Reflecting on the previous chambers that were filled with darkness, there was no light. There was no presence of God or His goodness. This was the lie. I had deceived myself.

I John 1:6 *If we say that we have fellowship with him, and walk in darkness, we lie, and do not the truth:....*

I closed my eyes and begin to pray.

Jesus I repent of lies in my heart. Satan is the Father of lies and I have allowed him to enter my heart. Lord I ask you to forgive me for speaking lies, believing lies, and hearing lies that bring deception. God, You are a Spirit and I must worship You in Spirit and in truth. Please forgive me Jesus. I repent for not speaking the truth in love. Forgive me for my sin, transgression and iniquity. Cleanse me with Your blood of this spirit of lying and every sin of my tongue. Create in me a clean heart and renew a right spirit within me. This spirit will not live in me any longer. Jesus, cleanse me of all unrighteousness with Your pure blood. I ask You to restore this chamber of my heart.

I did not have to wait long. The restoration was immediate. I opened my eyes to see a floor harp. It was a harp for worship. The harp reminded me of David –a true worshiper. Since the lies were gone from my heart, I could now worship the Father of Lights in Spirit and in Truth. This was now the Harp & Worship Chamber.

When I was a child, dancing and music filled my life in some form. I remember the first time I danced in front of a crowd. I led my kindergarten class at the auditorium of the city's university. We danced to *"Jeremiah was a bullfrog...."* This would be the beginning of a series of singing and dancing performances. In the 1970s, my sister and I would watch "Soul Train" on Saturday mornings for the latest dance and songs. I remember how I enjoyed participating in talents shows along with family and friends. I loved to dance and had no problem dancing with or without a partner.

Dancing is deeply rooted in my father's family, but singing is the heartbeat of my mother's family. The Lord blessed me with a passion to use both to worship Him. My mother faithfully took us to church and we participated in the choir. If her family got together, someone was going to sing and play the piano. I was about 13 years old when my mother purchased a piano for our home. In hindsight, this was also my gift from God. My life was radically changed with music. I found an outlet of expression for my muted soul. I would spend hours developing the skills to play and I soon began writing songs.

Dance is an expression of emotions that has always given a calm, soothing, quietness to my soul. Although I had been teaching children the expression of dance publicly, there was passion surging within my soul to dance before the Lord that could only be expressed privately, in the dark, under the canopy of heaven. It was here in the secluded places, I learned to dance with all my might before the Lord, who did not despise my offering of worship. About 2004, a dear woman named Barbara gave me my first worship flag. A year later, I was given a silk fire flag by another worshiper. These were gifts from the Lord I would not have known how to obtain. The Lord activated another area of worship that is still growing in creativity of designing and making silk flags.

There were many encounters with the Lord during these rendezvous, but I would like to share what happened a particular night. Because I did not want anyone to see me or interrupt my worship, I would go to empty baseball fields or parking lots late at night. Although I knew the risk of being outside alone, my greater yearning was to release the praise I had inside to glorify the Lord and display my love for Him. God was always faithful to protect me. I recall one night I was worshiping with the flags and expressing my unbridled love in dance when I looked up at the clear night sky. I saw the face of Jesus in the form of clouds. His eyes were closed as He smelled the vapor of my worship like incense rising from the altar. I could see the pleasure on His face and I experienced the joy of His presence. It would be over 10 years before I would share the magnitude of my private unfettered worship publicly. I was no longer afraid of what people thought because under the canopy of darkness the Lord was creating a worshiper after His heart while He was healing my heart.

After my husband died, I was very overwhelmed with multiple concerns. I remember asking the Lord if I should see a therapist because I had cycle of depression from the traumatic events in my life. I heard the Lord say, *"If you praise Me, I'll heal you."* That is what I did. I worshiped the Lord with song, dance, and banners. I can testify that He not only healed me, but elevated my worship to a new level. I recall one time I asked for songs from Heaven and He sent an angel to give me the song on a scroll. This has happened several times and I felt the Lord wanted me to share this song to compliment this book. I am sharing some of the beautiful songs inspired by the Lord on my worship CD titled "Spontaneous". The songs are the expressions of reformation of each chamber of my heart. I pray it will inspire you to experience your own heart journey to bring healing as you worship, dance and sing unto the Lord.

In the outreach program for children living in high risk environment, the art of dance is used to help children to find hope and healing through creative expression. For a variety of reasons, the children we serve are often experiencing some form of emotional brokenness, which can manifest in extreme behaviors, isolation, promiscuity, and unhealthy relationships. My hope is that their expression through creative arts can become a gateway to encounter the presence and delight of the Lord as His creation. Creative expression encourages transparency as we practice trust and build social skills that lead to meaningful human interactions. Our vision rests on the truth of scripture:

Heart Makeover

To appoint unto them that mourn in Zion, to give unto them beauty for ashes, the oil of joy for mourning, the garment of praise for the spirit of heaviness; that they might be called trees of righteousness, the planting of the LORD, that he might be glorified. Isaiah 61:3

This is what the Lord did for me when He gave me the instruments of worship over the years. He taught me how to worship through my pain with a sacrifice of praise. As I was studying this passage of scripture, the Holy Spirit shared these nuggets of truth.

Jesus gave me beauty for *ashes of despair of a lonely broken heart that seemed beyond repair.* However, *in our greatest brokenness is the chance to display Jesus' greatest beauty. Beauty is who Jesus is as He is clothed in garments of majesty.*

He showed me that oil purifies that mind and brings healing. Oil is a symbol of holiness and purity that He brings to those called by His name for purpose and destiny. Oil is always applied to the head as it is found in scripture running down from Aaron's beard. In contrast, *mourning causes physical and mental anguish that is why minds must be purified.*

In a vision the Lord showed me a garment of praise. The best way to describe it is a long sleeve blue and white robe with tiny bells all over it. The Lord shared *"It is a constant reminder of my fruitfulness to those who love Me, whose hearts are tender to worship Me wherever they go… In My presence is liberty and joy. That is why praise is so important to set the captive free. They are burden down with cares. They are burden down with burdens I did not give them…consumed by the world's affection. Many of my people have heavy burdens they try to bear alone. When they come to Me with their problems crying for help, this is what I tell them- Worship Me. This spirit (of heaviness) comes to bind my people up with anger, anxiety, fear and anguish. The spirit of heaviness my child weighs on the heart of man in such a great way that it grieves my Spirit.*

I asked the Lord to show me the spirit of heaviness. He showed me a person walking with flesh or another person carried around their neck on both shoulders. If you can imagine that you had to carry someone on your shoulder day and night without rest. This is a burden. Then Lord had me read Psalms 61. You can read the entire Psalm, but I want to highlight verse 2: *From the end of the earth will I cry unto thee, when my heart is overwhelmed: lead me to the rock that is higher than I.* (KJV)

In the 1828 Webster's Dictionary, overwhelmed means to overspread or crush beneath something violent and weighty; to immerse and bear down; or to put over. I think you get the message the spirit of heaviness disheartens God's people by causing us to feel discouraged, demoralized and lose spirit.

I am blessed to experience worship in a place of intimacy with the

Lord that brings healing. I believe it is a gift of God to pass on the joy of worship that brings healing to these children. I am so grateful to see children who were angry, isolated or have poor social skills be transformed as they are enveloped in the presence of the Lord. Many of them have accepted Jesus in their heart after a worship experience and are bringing their siblings, relatives and friends to classes. Bless the Lord!

Heart Makeover

Chamber 7

The Throne Room

Isaiah 14:13 *For thou hast said in thine heart, I will ascend into heaven, I will exalt my throne above the stars of God: I will sit also upon the mount of the congregation, in the sides of the north:*

When I was drawing a picture of my heart and dividing the seven rooms on the notepad, I heard the Holy Spirit describe the 7th chamber. He said *"This is the Throne Room"*. I placed this room at the very end of the hall in the center. I placed a crown over the entrance to distinguish it from the other chambers. The throne room is always the place where one who has authority and influence sits to reign. I wondered who or what would be sitting in this place designed for the Lord of my life.

I opened the door to a dimly lit room. The sight of a dark horse rearing up defiantly on two feet faced me. He was in the left corner of the room. I knew this was the one I had heard about. This was the thing that started this entire search for truth. The dark horse rearing up repeatedly without hesitation represented <u>my unbroken will</u>. I spoke to the horse. *"You will calm down."* It continued to buck and rear up. I intensified my tone. *"You will be broken."* The horse continued to raise up his front legs and move them in a boxing like manner. He was not giving in easily, and stubbornly stood almost upright to fight against me. I commanded the horse by saying, *"You will submit."* Finally, the horse lowered its legs and galloped in circles within a small round pen in the corner of the throne room. I was comfortable enough that the horse, representing my will, had been broken for the moment. I was able to turn my focus away from the horse to continue to explore the large dimly lit room.

I looked straight ahead and noticed a set of stairs leading to a large square platform. I observed an high back chair that was obviously the throne for the king of my heart to rule and reside. Oh my! I was shocked and confused because there sat on this beautiful high backed chair was a small black monkey with a banana in its mouth. When I looked at it, it jumped off the chair, ran down off the platform and went to the right corner of the throne room. What was this about? Was this some evolution theory about me coming from a monkey?

I patiently observed the monkey's behavior and it finally made sense. The Spirit of the Lord gave me insight that this creature represented foolishness. According to the 1828 Webster's Dictionary, the word "foolish" literally describes one being void of understanding, sound judgment or discretion. Webster's relates to "foolish" in scripture as wicked, sinful, acting without regard to the divine law and glory, or to one's own eternal happiness. The Bible refers to people such as the foolish Galatians (Gal 3:1); foolish conversations that should be avoided (2 Timothy 2:23) and foolish behaviors (1 Timothy 6:9) that result from being without understanding.

I knew what had to be done. This room was out of control and out of order. All these things had accumulated with time. I bowed my head and prayed. This prayer was not recorded and I have not tried to recreate it, but it was a prayer of desperation out of my soul.

Divine Restoration

***James 4:7-8** Submit yourselves therefore to God. Resist the devil, and he will flee from you. Draw nigh to God, and he will draw nigh to you. Cleanse your hands, ye sinners; and purify your hearts, ye double minded.*

After the prayer, I immediately looked up to see Him. Jesus was sitting up on the platform in the high-back chair. My true King and Lord was restored on the throne of my heart. I stood in awe as I gazed as His beauty and splendor. However, He did not return to the throne room alone. I noticed a beautiful and radiant woman stood on the floor to the right of the throne. She was clothed in a floor length white dress radiant with purity. I noticed her hair styled in an updo and she wore a diamond studded tiara on her head. The Holy Spirit instinctively revealed her name. Her name was Wisdom. She had now replaced the

Heart Makeover

foolish monkey that I saw running away to the right side of the Throne.

Proverbs 9:1 *Wisdom hath builded her house, she hath hewn out her seven pillars:*

In the Throne room Wisdom is adorned as an eloquent queen standing in the courts of the Lord. It is Wisdom who has established the house that is perfect and complete to welcome guest that will be disciples. In Proverbs 9, Wisdom prepares a feast and sends invitations by her maidens who are pure and undefiled. The invitations are given to the simple who want understanding.

Proverbs 9:4-6 *Whoso is simple, let him turn in hither: as for him that wanteth understanding, she saith to him, Come, eat of my bread, and drink of the wine which I have mingled.6 Forsake the foolish, and live; and go in the way of understanding.*

I knew that my life had been consumed with foolishness and simple-minded ways. The Lordship of Jesus brought Wisdom to my heart so that I could have a new mind. He did not despise my need for help and gave me understanding that I had been living foolishly, but now Wisdom would lead me.

Wisdom's instruction in Prov 9:6 is to forsake foolishness and live.

Webster's defines "forsake" as to renounce or turn away from entirely All of the things in my life that had led to a heart of darkness and disorder must be abandoned. As you have been on this journey with me through my heart, you have witnessed that wherever there was repentance, the current occupant was evicted, but the room was never left vacant. Each chamber was filled with light and purpose. The reward of Wisdom is a long healthy life.

Unlike the previous renovations that removed all the animal related symbolisms – the snake and lizard- the throne room makeover was different. I saw King Jesus restored on the throne of my heart with Wisdom to replace the foolish monkey king. However, the strong horse representing my will remained in the round pen established in the room. Although the horse was calm and submitting to the reigning authority, I could see that my will never dies. My will is never replaced nor does it disappear.

I realized that the horse-my will-is always present before the King as a submitted servant. This leads to obedience to the authority of the King who rules the heart with Wisdom. This means that when I don't obey it is because I have made a choice to follow my will. We always have the potential to disobey God by not submitting our will. This is why we must daily seek the will of God in prayer and repentance. Unless we are drawing close to God…we are drifting away—there is no neutral place.

Heart Makeover

The 7th Chamber reveals the recklessness that effects every area of our life when ruled by foolishness and the righteousness that is revealed in our mind, will, body, and relationship with others as we let Wisdom instruct us in submission to the Lord Jesus Christ. This is the truth of salvation – God gives us the choice. He doesn't want us to love or serve Him out of obligation. I believe this is why He gives us the freedom to act upon, direct, or submit our hearts' desire to please God or to please ourselves.

John 5:30 *I can of mine own self do nothing: as I hear, I judge: and my judgment is just; because I seek not mine own will, but the will of the Father which hath sent me.*

Proverbs 9:10 *The fear of the Lord is the beginning of wisdom: and the knowledge of the holy is understanding.*

Heart Makeover

Divine Direction

Psalms 90:12 *So teach us to number our days, that we may apply our hearts unto wisdom.*

I sat in awe of what God had done in this time with Him. I had carefully labeled each room to reflect the beauty that the Lord had restored with such grace and tenderness. I asked for the Lord's guidance in how to maintain the room's intent and fulfill the purpose of each room. The Holy Spirit spoke with greater clarity of the purpose, assignment and direction of each area of my heart. Just as He had led me through the process in sequence to restore order, He took me back through the each chamber in order from one to seven.

The first chamber was now called the Love Chamber. It relates to my relationship with God and sharing Him with others in ministry. The Holy Spirit responded: *Let the love of My light shine in You in the outreach. My hands are stretched out to My people to come back to Me. Bring them My daughter. Bring them to My open arms of love.*

The second chamber was now called the Romance-Marriage Chamber. *As I told you, I ordained this marriage. It is of Me. I will bring and restore your heart with laughter, love, and gentleness/kindness to one another.* (A snake is at our feet. I tell him and ask the angel to take him out. He beats him down some more and removes it) I declare no more coming between us. The Lord continues... *I will restore your womanhood to its fullness. Build him (husband) up with the words of your lips.* I ask the Holy Spirit, Do I compliment him? He responds "Yes, encourage him. It is easy. Just follow My lead."

The third chamber was now called the Writing-Career Chamber. I hear the Father laugh. *I have put many books in you that will change lives. Let Me show you how to express the will of My heart for My people to be released from fear, unforgiveness, and madness/sadness of their souls. Start immediately when you get the software. It will bring great delight.* I ask, "Is this a book?" *Yes. Write it down with clarity. I will restore your memory. It will bring truth to the heart of My people.*

The fourth chamber was now called the Servant-Giving Chamber. *The Giving room is where you serve. You will serve My people who are downcast, afflicted, and wounded spiritually, physically, mentally. They are unaware of their wounds, but I will give you surgeon's hands to heal. Yes, heal them in My Name. Trust Me now. It won't be long...*

The fifth chamber was now called the Body-Health Chamber. *Your body is the temple of The Holy Spirit. Do not abuse it with food. I have much in store to restore your health with brightness as the morning sun. Disease and sickness will have no place in your heart.*

The sixth chamber was now called the Harp-Worship Chamber. *Write songs. I delight in the songs of your heart to Me. I will give you new instruments and songs of praise. Don't limit your ability in Me. Sing in the earth. Sing songs to fill the heavens of My endless worth my daughter. Give Me praise.*

The seventh chamber was now called the Throne Room. *Seek Me daily. In My presence is the fullness of joy, and at My right hand are pleasures forevermore. Seek Me, My face before the sun rises. I will show you why. This is necessary. Prove Me now says God. I will surely bless you.*

Caution

You may go as you please, but be careful not to spend a lot of time in any one room. They all need maintaining. I am trusting you to do this in My Name. Be sure to spend time with Me.

I know how I have a tendency to get out of balance. I will do something and become consumed with completing it until it drains the life from me. Then I get very little sleep and then sit it down for a season.

The next day I spent restructuring my life. I now knew what I was called to do and what areas needed to be maintained to give direction, focus, and fullness. I knew my life had become chaotic because I lacked the structure. I returned to writing out things to do before starting each day to give focus to what was important and necessary.

Stop the Wandering

Psalms 119:10 *With my whole heart have I sought thee: O let me not wander from thy commandments.*

The psalmist Robert Robinson wrote the song, *"Come thy Fount of Every Blessing"* in 1758. The last refrain says...

Prone to wander
Lord I feel it
Prone to leave the God I love
Here's my heart
O take and seal it
Seal it for thy courts above

How many times has my heart wandered? It is never intentionally, but it is just as easy to wander when there is no fixed focus. **Psalm 23:3** *He restoreth my soul: he leadeth me in the paths of righteousness for his name's sake.*

Matthew Henry explains in his commentary that *"No creature will lose itself sooner than a sheep, so apt is it to go astray, and then so unapt to find the way back. The best saints are sensible of their proneness to go astray like lost sheep; they miss their way, and turn aside into by-paths; but when God shows them their error, gives them repentance, and brings them back to their duty again, He restores the soul; and, if He did not do so, they would wander endlessly and be undone."*

This "wandering heart syndrome" has its place recorded time and time again in The Bible. The book of Judges shows after the death of Joshua, the children of Israel continued the cycle of wandering away from God by not killing the Canaanites, intermarriages, and worshiping idols. This became a snare and led them into oppression. God raised up judges again and again...you get the idea.

When reading the history of the mistakes others have made, it is easy to judge and say what we would have done. There are many Christians who can say their hearts have never wandered away from God. However, I would dare to say there remains many Christians who have struggled with snares of idolatry that have caused a wandering away from God. Jesus is our High Priest, King, and our Shepherd. He is full of grace and truth to draw our wandering hearts to The One who loves us.

Psalms 57:7 *My heart is fixed, O God, my heart is fixed: I will sing and give praise.*

The Psalmist proclaims a praise and singing because the heart is now fixed. Jesus has come in and not only divinely cleaned the clutter of sin but divinely restored the heart to its purpose and strength.

The things that were covered up, out of order and cluttered are now exposed, destroyed, removed, and organized. The Spirit of God now occupies each chamber with life and light for fruitfulness.

My heart is fixed, O God! my heart is fixed. The context of fixed means "standing erect," "established" or "strengthened". My heart is erect and strengthened. What is the purpose of every chamber of the heart being fixed? The Psalmist answers... *to sing and give praise.*

When I was about 26 years old, I went through the phase "What is the purpose of my life?" It consumed me. I felt I never got an answer because I was trying to figure it out through human reasoning. It has been over twenty years since that turmoil set me on a journey to find the answers. I am thankful for the Lord answering many of my prayers and leading me through the search. I realize the journey is never really over since in our relationship with the Lord we become lifelong learners.

I pray it will not take you twenty years to ask The Heart Maker what is your purpose? He is willing and ready to reveal it to you personally. If you have read this book and made it to this page, I believe your answer is clear...you are ready.

Entering the Chambers Inventory Sheet

As you read through the book I pray you are provoked to ask the Holy Spirit to guide you through the Chambers of your own heart. For some, this may take hours and others a few days. It may be painful and liberating all at the same time. As you sit before the Lord, simply ask Him:

Lord Jesus, I am seeking truth. I now am ready for you to reveal the deep truth of what lives in the chambers of my heart. My heart is open to You. You know things about me that I don't even know about myself. You know the things hidden away that I don't want anyone else to know. Today, I surrender to You Lord to create in me a clean heart and renew a right spirit within me. I thank You for Your abiding love for me as You walk with me through this journey. Amen.

I have designed these workbook pages to help you navigate through your journey. There are four sections for each chamber.

The Chamber Revealed.

This worksheet is an area for you to write down everything The Holy Spirit reveals. Don't worry about it being orderly. Put it all down. It may make sense later. Record what you perceived through your senses - see, hear, smell, touch, taste and think. If you are not able to capture all of the details of your experience, do not become anxious. Focus on the main points and fill the details in later as The Holy Spirit brings them back to remembrance.

The Chamber Prayer Of Repentance Or Gratitude

This worksheet provides an area where you may place the highlights of your prayer. My intent is not to get you in a 'model' prayer, but after you have prayed out of your heart, simply place key words and later include scriptures pertaining to the area revealed. Unfortunately, all of my rooms need major repentance, but you may be blessed with a chamber clean and operating in its divine intent. Praise God! Celebrate with a prayer of thanksgiving.

The Chamber Restored

This worksheet is an area to record the details of your "divine makeover". Describe the change and how you feel in the room. I observed during this process that the things I always enjoyed doing were reaffirmed as God's divine purpose for me. The restoration process brought clarity and confirmation to the "puzzle pieces" I had collected over the years through dreams, visions, prophesy, or prayer.

The Chamber Applied

The second part of this restoration is application. What is The Holy

Spirit saying? Where and how does the Lord want me to apply this spiritual transformation in reality? The hardest thing with truth is not knowing where and when to apply it to our lives. This is where Wisdom gives understanding. I learn to ask the Lord for as many details as He will share. This is not because I do not trust Him, but it is because I have a relationship where I want to please Him by walking it out in obedience, in His time and way.

For example, you may have a chamber for teaching and you ask the Holy Spirit for His plan. He may direct you to go to an elementary school, take government training, teach as a college professor or become a Sunday school teacher. Are there implied tasks to prepare for the application? If I am going to teach college level math, this will require I obtain a college degree.

May I interject here that I have seen my life get spiritually out of balance because I refused to do the practical natural things. In 2010, the Spirit showed me it was a season God was preparing and placing His people in position through natural and spiritual training processes. We see examples of this in The Bible with Joseph, Esther, and Moses. Since there is a process, we must submit to the process and purposes of God to fulfill the plan through His provision. In 2013, the Lord revealed that this was a season of birthing. He showed me He was birthing forth ministries with His anointing, protection, and provision.

I encourage you not to compare your results with mine because the purpose of the exercise is to simply allow The Spirit of God to reveal truth. What appears in the physical is not indicative of the truth of the Spirit. Only God knows our heart, our motives, our intents, and thoughts. Let God's Word be the two edge sword *"piercing even to the dividing asunder of soul and spirit, and of the joints and marrow, and is a discerner of the thoughts and intents of the heart."*

Enjoy your journey.

Chamber Worksheets

The following worksheets contain steps needed to address areas on your journey. You may use one word descriptions, pictures, scriptures and/or narratives to help you remember your experience. Be patient with yourself as The Holy Spirit ministers His truths. It is worth it! You may copy these worksheets or create your own.

Heart Makeover

The Chamber Revealed

The Chamber Prayer of Repentance

The Chamber Restored

The Chamber Applied

The Chamber Revealed

The Chamber Prayer of Repentance

The Chamber Restored

The Chamber Applied

Heart Makeover

<u>The Chamber Revealed</u>

<u>The Chamber Prayer of Repentance</u>

<u>The Chamber Restored</u>

<u>The Chamber Applied</u>

The Chamber Revealed

The Chamber Prayer of Repentance

The Chamber Restored

The Chamber Applied

Heart Makeover

The Chamber Revealed

The Chamber Prayer of Repentance

The Chamber Restored

The Chamber Applied

The Chamber Revealed

The Chamber Prayer of Repentance

The Chamber Restored

The Chamber Applied

Heart Makeover

<u>The Chamber Revealed</u>

<u>The Chamber Prayer of Repentance</u>

<u>The Chamber Restored</u>

<u>The Chamber Applied</u>

I Speak To Myself:
Encouraging Words for Children

This book seeks to affirm children in their value and identity because we are "fearfully and wonderfully we are made." We have the power to be our greatest encourager as we speak to ourselves the words God speaks over us. This is an excellent book to build self-esteem and to encourage children in their daily walk toward purpose and destiny.

Raindrops of Mercy:
Comforting Words for Children

In her second book, Raindrops of Mercy, she draws from her painful childhood experiences. Clem wrote this book to let children know they are not alone in their pain. She shares the comfort and healing of Jesus Christ she received when she learned how to forgive and live... because we all need mercy.

About the Author

Clem "Liley" McConnell is an author, poet, psalmist, and entrepreneur. As a result of emotional brokenness, her passion is to help heal and restore children in their identity, purpose, and acceptance through Christ. She combines her spontaneous creativity, arts, and love for worship as tools to bring freedom and joy. Liley has spent over 16 years encouraging children in various churches, schools, and organizations. After the death of her husband, the Lord changed Clem's name to Liley to represent how her life would blossom in this new season. She is the founder of Lion of Judah Ministries which uses expressive art to engage children in the inner city.

About the Music

Liley shares her love for music and songwriting that has brought her healing throughout her life. This debut companion album, *"Spontaneous"*, is composed of songs from heaven to enhance your heart journey as you read *"Heart Makeover"*. The songs relate to each chamber of Liley's heart journey. She encourages you to worship the Lord as He heals your heart in the deep places. May you be inspired to sing your own song.

NOTES

NOTES